6 Creative Habits

That Form A

Wonderful Environment And

Add More Money

In Your Pocket!

A Simple Guide!

By: Anthony A. Jackson

TABLE OF CONTENTS

Protect Your Community

Chapter 1

PROTECT YOUR COMMUNITY

Protecting the community, you live in comes in different forms, actions, and deeds that portray a decent gesture from my point of view. The same can be assumed for other aspects that may involve showing a protected nature towards such as, close relatives or a personal connection to an individual. Let's shift back to the subject of protecting the community a person lives in. Over the past years, numerous people produced their ideas, opinions, and beliefs of how something should be done and probably still incorporate those same ideas, opinions, and beliefs without the upgrade. Now, a sure method of innovation is presented and a relaxed approach on protection of communities is key. Safely disposing of hazardous chemical substances that are in households. Upkeep maintenance of the area that a person lives on which can include cutting the lawn weekly. Last, minimize harmful vehicle emissions to travel to important places instead of unnecessary trips. Implementing these three practices consistently can bring steady change, a healthier and cleaner environment, and a chance to witness a beautiful community.

DISPOSING HAZARDOUS CHEMICAL SUBSTANCES

Recycling unsafe chemical substances speak for itself, which should be handled with care. How a person carries out the process can be another aspect. Most households will likely be exposed to different types of chemical substances that have a sign labeled with caution. Simple tasks can assist in shrinking the number of chemical substances that accidentally enter the community people live in. Therefore, properly throwing away spray cans such as insect killer into solid waste containers can create a difference even if it sounds insignificant. Consequently, every sincere action counts, which also allows the chemicals that become restricted from getting into the water system of a community a plus. Not only will this have positive encouragements, it will also create a better environment.

UPKEEP MAINTENANCE

Upkeep maintenance can be done on objects that dwell in the world today. From vehicles, homes, and pets, and even the body, need upkeep, maintenance done to it for longevity over time. The subject discussed is lawn maintenance, which can be done year-round. Modest approaches such as cutting the grass, trimming hedges, raking leaves and picking up sticks all support the consistent beauty of the community a person lives in. The area may be your land or not the responsibility of other people, however, keeping it up and groomed are thoughtful methods that can help limit debris that may also travel through drains. Cutting grass can be a hot job, although it needs to be done. Most large businesses participate in professional lawn care and provide excellent service that implies safe environmental practices. The same principles can be duplicated and reinforced in homes to ensure that households are aware and educated regarding safer practices. Again, crucial information that can be gained on the topic includes victory in keeping living areas clean.

MINIMIZE HARMFUL VEHICLE EMISSIONS

This topic can be intriguing and probably a not so pleasant one either. Approximately, anyone can say, that they like driving to and from wherever they feel like. I know a few local trips are necessary, especially if the location of a near dollar general is close. This is automatic and temptation will win if the strength to withdraw is overwhelming. Another place can be Walmart often for just a couple of items. After that, those couple of items turn into three, four, or five items and its time to leave. Frequent rides to the grocery store can increase dangerous vehicle emissions as well, so this is another part that can be included in the overall picture of protecting one's community. The picture is to illustrate how unconsciously, people form decisions to drive to places often without a need to. So, trying to approach the mindset of limiting back and forth travel to a location and from a location is the point. The idea sounds probably restricted but trying to lessen travel to more specific places and frequencies such as the post office, dollar store, grocery store, gas station, Walmart, and other places two or three times a week. This can improve and eliminate a vast majority of toxic fumes that come from vehicles daily in the community of residence. With the participation of everyone, the job can be done and create a cleaner atmosphere in the community and worldwide.

PROTECT YOUR COMMUNITY

Overall, protecting the community a person lives in is paramount, starts at home, and brings about change in a positive way. The nonchalant tasks can sound a bit lame, such as disposing hazardous chemical substances, upkeep, maintenance of the area that you live on, and minimizing harmful vehicle emissions. All include a simple step to improving the essence of the community and therefore is a must consider when this is at stake. I challenge every individual to take one simple task and gradually include that into the daily routine one is accustomed to. Eventually, it becomes second nature and habit. Creating laid back habits like this is probably better than incorporating the complete opposite and not getting nowhere. So, lets come together and practice, practice, practice! The communities are anticipating these lively gestures for their protection, let's give them that!

Challenge
Global Climate Change
Chapter 2

GLOBAL CLIMATE CHANGE

Global climate change can be a debatable subject. For many years, the phenomena breaths opinionated beliefs, differences, statistics, and facts that allow prevalence in modern time. Sound research and studies conclude that global climate change can be real and that several of the effects are caused by human interactions on Earth. Evidence from scientists and other professionals also present that over the years, the Earth's temperatures, oceans, atmosphere, and land have changed negatively due to the actions of people. To decrease this type of negative impact on the Earth, effective measures can be taken to ensure the longevity of Earth for generations to come. Setting local emission goals can be an effective method that can limit harmful emissions into the atmosphere. Second, consider the decision to stand against climate change and find worth in that decision. Last, apply the knowledge and research that you have gained on the topic in everyday life. These three methods sound difficult but applying them brings perfection and consistently doing the actions overall decreases dangerous emissions and other harmful objects that are put into the environment.

SETTING LOCAL EMISSION GOALS

Setting local emission goals is a tough task at hand that can be accomplished with initiative and the right mindset. When discussing this topic, the point focuses on towns, cities, villages, and communities developing emission goals to govern their areas. Leaders such as the mayor, town council, can create and accept ideas from anyone that has an interest in limiting harmful emissions. By doing this, it gives a direct approach to monitor the emissions that enter the atmosphere. Not only will this help, it will also allow people in a community setting to participate and actively engage in the cause. Starting home first can be a good start in hopes that the initiative will bring forth a positive influence towards other communities, cities, towns, and villages to apply the same principles or methods when improving local emission standards. Change will not happen overnight, however, a sincere effort to form and apply emission goals, less toxic fumes will be protruded into the atmosphere and decrease climate change significantly.

MAKE DECISIONS OF WORTH

Facing decisions in life seem to be the most difficult aspect when done. We accompany several throughout everyday life and constantly challenged at every angle. However, deciding towards global climate change can also bring a mixed feeling especially if one has no valuable knowledge in the subject. To ease tension, I recommend including a sense of worth behind decision making. For example, research and understand the issues when dealing with global climate change and the negative effects it has on humans, animals, Earth, and the environment. Then realize if the actions taken against global climate change, embrace worth, time and energy to invest, overall. This can lessen the anxiety that may arise when deciding to stand against climate change. Also, consider not only the present but future generations to come. Ask yourself this question, should I stand now or put global climate change on the back burner with the possibility of future generations inhabiting an unclean Earth?

APPLY KNOWLEDGE OF GLOBAL CLIMATE CHANGE

Now that knowledge and research exist on the worldwide issue of global climate change, applying and implementing the same information can be vital. What benefit can that knowledge be if not applied in real-life situations? Simple steps and tasks can be carried out to assist in minimizing harmful effects on the environment, ecosystems, habitats, and preventing the harsh effects of climate change. One sure way to apply knowledge of climate change is decreasing carbon dioxide emissions that come from vehicles. Concrete evidence from scientists suggests that this can be a main aspect of increasing climate change that causes heavy emissions into the atmosphere. So, decreasing transportation can be a way to lessen carbon dioxide emissions. Another modest approach can be to have an awareness of the actions brought on the environment around you. If doing something such as dumping harmful chemicals down drains, throwing trash on the ground instead of recycling, or cutting trees down and harms the environment, then I would consider limiting these actions. Negative outcomes may not be seen instantly, however, potential harm can be done to the environment and induces the concept of global climate change to a certain extent.

GLOBAL CLIMATE CHANGE

Overall, a stand against global climate change is a positive action that can bring about successful results. One person is not responsible for the entire persona of climate change. It takes towns, communities, and cities to come together and implement plans of action that can make a difference and decrease the damage done to the earth. This will influence and hopefully spark attention on a state and national level spreading the news around other countries. As mentioned before, setting local emission goals, making wise decisions on climate change, and applying basic knowledge about climate change in real-world scenarios, are just basic principles for a solid stand against the issue. These same ideas need to be upheld in a moral way that allows everyone to participate diligently. Eventually, consistent actions of people will create change and defeat the overwhelming climate change topic we face today.

Safeguard Water Resources
Chapter 3

SAFEGUARD WATER RESOURCES

Water can be a precious substance that encompasses a large portion of the Earth. For years, people have depended on water for a variety of daily tasks and routines. Water connects to humans, not only for ordinary home tasks, the very essence of decent health depends solely on water and its superb qualities. When mentioning water, safeguarding this prized commodity can be important. However, many steps and procedures can be done to ensure clean water presence often and not contaminated. Moreover, one step can be to decrease actions that potentially harm water resources such as, farming practices that utilize hazardous pesticide chemicals that run into drains. Another unique consideration that brings forth positive results relates to properly disposing of harmful chemicals. Finally, protecting water resources can start at residential locations such as, municipalities that focus on clean water initiatives. Accordingly, all strategic plans can accompany fruitful outcomes when implemented at a high level. Consequently, the objective decreases the amount of contamination that poses harm to water resources and working together as a team can accomplish this goal.

DECREASE HARMFUL AGRICULTURAL PRACTICES

The farming industry is prominent in the world today and is a major source for food humans eat daily. Fresh produce in the form of plants, meat, poultry, dairy, and fruits are supplied by the farming industry and to many individuals throughout the world. These vital sources are the very nutritional foundations of prolonged good health and including them in daily eating habits is paramount. Research and studies from nutritionists have also concluded that the proper intake of mainly fresh produce that is naturally organic is probably the best option. The process of growing, cultivating, and packaging to the markets is not seen from consumers most of the time, but discussing it can be another topic of concern. The issue of farming methods that include pesticides, insecticides, and fertilizers pose a threat to humans because of consumption. Although these chemicals are needed to control pests, decreasing the use of such chemicals can also lessen the amount of exposure to humans in the long run. Forming and generating possible alternatives to cultivate such as, utilizing safer methods that include nontoxic and dangerous substances can be done. This will create a more environmentally friendly idea of limiting pesticides, insecticides, and fertilizer use that meets water resources and can prove to be a helpful approach when the health of the environment and humans are at stake.

PROPER DISPOSAL OF HARMFUL CHEMICALS

Disposing harmful chemicals can be a trying task at hand. Face it, no one pays attention or shows a huge concern when getting rid of substances that are harmful to the environment and people. Consequently, most tend to dispose of chemicals of this nature readily into the environment without seeking proper ways to go about the process. This thought process and action has been evaluated by professional environmentalists, ecologists, scientists, and others to be the main reason behind the pollution of major water resources, the environment, and human health. Nevertheless, simple steps can be done to prevent this type of occurrence from happening and create a better shield of protection for prized water resources. One can easily take hazardous chemical substances to nearby facilities that govern and properly dispose of them. This ensures that none of the chemicals are thrown into the environment. Also, realizing the actions of everyday activities that may include the use of hazardous chemicals that can come from changing the oil in a vehicle, dangerous chemicals that generate from large industrial plants, and many other sources. Again, finding ways to diminish these types of actions not only lessens the use of harmful chemicals, however, it gives the water resources that provide civilization with pristine value a better chance of cleanliness.

APPLYING MUNICIPALITY CLEAN WATER INITIATIVES

Most towns, cities, and communities have a local municipality that provides water to its residents. For years, the formation of such facilities has also been proven to be efficient and effective, overall. Therefore, the main question at hand is safeguarding facilities and plants that provide clean water to customers daily. Nevertheless, many things can be done to guarantee that the quality of water resources is clean. Moreover, applying clean water initiatives and treating the water with proper chemicals that keep it clean is one practice. In addition, possible upgrades to the water system in the form of replacing old pipes with new ones. Setting the proposed plans and procedures that monitor the quality of the water daily. Another method that strikes attention is practicing these same initiatives in work-related areas to minimize possible contamination of water as well. This sounds difficult but can be done with the help of the local community, city, and town leaders. Seeking help even from state and government level organizations can assist in improving and maintaining good water quality. Accordingly, the central concern starts at the residential level and preventive actions that greatly eliminate the hazard to water resources can be a focal point. Starting at this level can make sure that water is clean when distributed to customers, the health of the people is thriving, and hopefully create an atmosphere that spreads clean water initiatives throughout the world.

SAFEGUARD WATER RESOURCES

Water can be a precious jewel and the source of it connects health to people in a vast number of ways. Everyday life depends on it from simple household tasks such as, washing dishes, washing clothes, taking a bath, and let's not forget drinking! The list can be long; however, the picture can be clear that water resources should be protected at a level of diligence. Unclean water happens to be a real and a true crisis throughout the world and in other countries. Health and wellness are affected tremendously when water resources are in danger or maybe contaminated by neglecting actions that harm them. So, the need to incorporate safer farming techniques, proper disposal of hazardous chemicals and substances, and apply clean water initiatives on a municipality level can be crucial. Change can happen overnight, nevertheless, effective collaboration from concerned people working together, community leaders, and others the job can be done. The overall health of the people and the environment will profit from doing these actions and continue to progress as time goes by.

Make Recycling Your Friend
Chapter 4

MAKE RECYCLING YOUR FRIEND

Most of the people in the world need a special friend that will be there for them in troubling times. Having a person of that nature who listens, cares and considers your feelings can be a good friend indeed. What can be intriguing and interesting would be to create and form a friendly relationship with recycling. Can this be possible??? However, this topic relates recycling to a friend and brings a creative idea that anyone can include in everyday life. When discussing friendship, one can embrace recycling in numerous ways to withdraw the overwhelming responsibility that recycling can bring. One method that can allow recycling to be a close friend can be including types of recycling in everyday life. Another interesting method that can form a close friendship with recycling relates to connecting with a local recycling facility. Learning and knowing about your friend signals understanding them better, so visiting a solid waste facility and becoming acquainted with personnel and the job that goes on at the facility can help build a close friendship with recycling from my point of view. Finally, apply recycling techniques in everyday life with simple tasks that can range from throwing plastic bottles in a recycling bin, or separating the trash for recyclables that are accumulated in a household. These three methods can spark a friendship with recycling and hopefully endures for a long time. With the help of residents and others, these three ideas can also create a pleasant atmosphere with friendly recycling as the main priority.

CREATING FRIENDSHIPS WITH RECYCLING

Friendship and recycling can be two different subjects to discuss, nevertheless, the idea of both strikes a different tone when connecting them as one unit. Friendship can be a wonderful experience, especially when the connection between the person is sincere and genuine. Many can say that friendship is part of a healthy lifestyle. Recycling takes another approach of the actions that can be required when doing recycling. Over the years, recycling has been pictured as an overwhelming task that is difficult to carry out. However, this is not the case. With new modern technology, recycling is simpler than ever. Lets picture linking the aspect of friendship and recycling together for a moment. From my point of view, one can easily incorporate recycling in everyday life. Taking a couple of empty bags or bins, labeling them for recycling, and placing them inside or outside of the residence one lives in can gradually form a friendship type connection with recycling instead of being a chore-based approach. The same principle can be applied to a municipality level to get the community a person can live in involved. This makes it easier for solid waste garbage trucks to dispose of the material at the waste facility. The idea is to keep recycling close like a friend as much as possible and again create a connection of care and love when doing an action of recycling.

VISITING LOCAL RECYCLING FACILITIES

Most towns, villages, cities, and communities have a local solid waste facility in the area. Depending on how far and the location of the solid waste facility is from the area one lives in can be an obstacle. Not having transportation to and from a facility that is responsible for recycling materials can be another problem. Simply neglecting the fact of how recycling may seem can hinder a visit to a facility. There could be variables that can deter an individual from visiting a local recycling facility, however, the awareness is to personally realize the importance of recycling and create a sound decision to form a trip to a local solid waste organization. Most select trips daily to and from places of necessity, therefore, making a trip to an important facility wouldn't hurt a bit. The trip can be rewarding or not, nevertheless, it allows you to become acquainted with the personnel that works at the location. You also have the chance to notice daily routine operations that happen every day when recycling takes place. Forming transactional relationships that can eventually lead to meaningful friendships is another positive outcome when visiting a recycling facility. You never know, someone might offer you a job if they notice the level of concern and interest in recycling you have. Accordingly, think about the visit and organize a trip to a local facility. Maybe the answers to unclear questions about recycling and the importance of it can be resolved with firsthand experience of people that work at solid waste facilities.

APPLY RECYCLING TECHNIQUES

Recycling can be important to the environment, human health, living, and nonliving organisms that dwell on the earth. The valuable knowledge obtained from recycling can also be a useful tool to utilize in everyday life. All the information gathered can be essential from a given standpoint. However, what good can the information gained from recycling be, if not applied in any type of daily activity that a person performs regularly? My perspective can simply inform that when applying the knowledge that you gain from reusing, reducing, and recycling, it can help improve understanding and connections on the idea of recycling. Simple routines that acquire a place in our lives that revolve around recycling can be in the form of variety and simple tasks. Throwing trash away in a disposable, recyclable container instead of throwing the trash on the ground can be one scenario. Hazardous waste usually thrown outside happens frequently, however, that can be properly done by disposing of in a hazardous waste container. These two examples are just a couple of issues that can be dealt with when recycling can be the focus. Although the actions occur at a normal rate, applying the knowledge increased by study and research can put a stop to the neglected and hazardous actions forced upon the environment, human health, home or community a person lives in.

MAKE RECYCLING YOUR FRIEND

Overall, recycling proves to be a good option when it limits the vast amount of danger that poses a threat to the environment, human health, and communities people live in. Accordingly, accountability of the actions a person does every day that considers a form of recycling is a major step in improving the complete concept of recycling. As mentioned earlier, including recycling in everyday life has the advantage of enabling a better community, town, village, or city. Moreover, the same can be said when a simple visit to a local solid waste or recycling facility is done with the intentions of gaining and connecting with the people that work at the location. Let's not forget that applying the knowledge learned from recycling and other sources of information need to be included in daily routines. The tasks may seem difficult to carry out, however, consistent and diligent actions towards recycling can hopefully create a healthier and safer environment. Consequently, when these three strategic methods are applied, the future of the earth will be cleaner for generations to come.

Form An Interesting Club

Chapter 5

FORM AN INTERESTING CLUB

The environment and nature are beautiful sights to appreciate every day. So, tackling the concepts of protecting the environment can be a different task at hand. However, the job is not difficult when help is at disposal. This topic talks about the formation of an interesting recycle club that can be organized by the people in the community one lives in. Forming a recycling club can be a laid-back job when residents have the same objective of protecting the environment. Moreover, gathering a few people together and creating a friendly based theme towards recycling is one method that can start an interesting club. Accordingly, when forming a club, be creative within the group to create an enjoyable environment! Projects can consist of making recycling rewarding with gifts, incentives, or tickets to movies for every positive action that is done when a person recycles. Another way to form an interesting club is to have parades that focus on the benefits of recycling. This can be done through schools located in the community, town, village, or city a person lives in. Nevertheless, it allows local schools, faculty, students, parents and the community to come together and be involved in a worthy cause to promote recycling at a parade. Consequently, forming an interesting club can bring about a significant change and create an overall atmosphere that allows everyone to feel like their actions towards recycling are worth the time and effort to protect the environment people live in.

GATHER PEOPLE WITH SAME VIEWPOINTS ABOUT RECYCLING

This can be a strenuous job when it comes to gathering people that have the same viewpoints about recycling. People simply are not caring enough about recycling and the advantages it brings towards the community a person lives in or the environment. So, choosing the right people may be challenged in the long run. However, a few people desire a change and difference when it comes to recycling and likely are close friends, family or relatives that may fit the description. Introduce the crucial issue of recycling to close friends, family members, and relatives to perceive if their interest is genuine. Expound the reason and the passion that is implicated in recycling and coming together to form an interesting club. Try to illustrate positive and enjoyable features that will happen when forming a club and not focus on the idea of recycling as something mundane. This will help initiate an interest and importantly understanding of the perception when creating a club. Also, be straightforward about the intentions of making a recycling club so that no one is left with the feeling of their actions having no value or meaning. Comprehending that one person will need help eventually and seeking that assistance from the right people will spark the minds of close friends, family members, and relatives.

ALLOWING CREATIVITY IN RECYCLING CLUB

Being creative with talent and gifts abides in people. However, applying that same creativity towards a recycling club can be another task at hand. Throughout life, people present and showcase their skills in multi-faceted ways. Moreover, painting, drawing, building, writing, and numerous other activities bring out the best creative skills one has ever seen. So, channel the same energy into a recycling club and create a lively atmosphere. In addition, ideas can stimulate from different sources to allow this club to flourish in a significant way. Nevertheless, one idea can create incentives such as movie tickets, trips, a cruise, and concerts. Accordingly, this allows the setting of the club to be driven by applying recycling techniques daily. Creating a pot of money each month for the person who recycles greater material within a month's time frame can be an idea. This can keep individuals determined to recycle when money can be involved! People need the money and a gesture that resembles this can be a plus when having the attention of people and the potential to win a pot of money! It even sounds intriguing! Another creative method allows a person to create a day off from the club. Though carrying out recycling habits can be a bit overwhelming and tiresome, however, a day off from activity can surely bring initiative within the club. So, implementing creativity into an interesting club can be a plus and promotes the active engagement from individuals.

HAVE RECYCLING PARADES

As we all know, parades are extravagant occurrences most of the time when everything goes well. However, many people journey to and from different locations just to accompany parades for the excitement. In addition, football season generates parades, basketball season has parades, homecoming, and cannot forget about Mardi Gras, which is probably the biggest parade in every location that commemorates the day. So, why not orchestrate a parade for a recycling club? Accordingly, the same idea and perception can be incorporated in the setting of the club parade. Constructing costumes such as recycling containers can be worn in the parade and allow people to put recyclable items into the containers for recycling. This allows people to become engrossed with the parade and permitting individuals to recycle at the same time. Nevertheless, designing trucks with logos that say recycle can enrich the atmosphere at the parade and while trucks are moving allows people to put recyclable objects into the backs of trucks. Again, making recycling easy while a parade is in function. Also take turns with individuals to participate in the parade every time it is developed in the town, village, city, or community you live in leaving no one feeling left out. The recycling parade can be formed rendering the need to recycle so that the intentions will not be weighed down by the excess application. Consequently, coming together, participating diligently, and having a sincere effort towards recycling can make the parade that much better.

FORM AN INTERESTING CLUB

Overall, studies, research, and sound information concerning recycling prove that the benefit outweighs the cost of damaging the environment. Moreover, it can be problematic for one person to manufacture a change on a subject that is in extreme need of attention. The focus can be to keep the community, town, village, or city one lives in unpolluted and healthy. With all the valuable information around the world at access, it can be done at a fast rate no one has seen before. As mentioned before in the text, gathering people together that have the same viewpoints on recycling can be one step. In addition, allowing creativity to flow into an interesting club can be a second step. Lastly, constructing recycling parades as needed can be the icing on the cake. However, just imagine harnessing these three principles in your community, town, village, or city. Ordinarily, think it over clearly and accommodate time to let it sink in. After that, ask yourself, can the protection of the environment be worthy? Will it be entertaining? What will I gain from it? Or maybe will applying the three methods create a healthier future for generations to come?

Setting Good Examples

Chapter 6

SETTING GOOD EXAMPLES

Setting beneficial examples comes in numerous forms. The real question can be concerned with examples of sincere, genuine, and not forced approaches when applied to recycle. However, anything in life, whether it's raising kids, conducting the identity of yourself to portray a decent person, being a leader in a position in life, requires a well-mannered example for people. Nevertheless, this subject focuses on ways to apply decent examples when recycling can be the objective. One might say, how can this be done when a simple task requires to pick up a piece of trash and put it into a recycling container? Well, consider this same thought and apply it with a sense of enthusiasm and appreciate the difference or encouragement it has on other people. In addition, several ways can show that a person can be sincere about setting moral examples when recycling. Moreover, one way that can show a respectable gesture towards recycling can be doing the procedure yourself consistently. Being consistent in noble habits or practices brings about worthy results eventually. Recycling consistently in everyday life allows others to recognize the pride, passion, and caring nature of the environment a person possesses. Consequently, the result, can be a valuable example and will influence others to perform at the same level.

SETTING GOOD EXAMPLES

Another way to show a suitable example of recycling is by incorporating the technique at the job a person works at. Moreover, this also allows coworkers and colleagues to have the opportunity to witness the action. Whether it's an undemanding job or on a corporate level, this can set a trend that can potentially proliferate across different spectrums of the world. As a result, it can also be contagious, and the focus can be on getting valuable information out there about recycling. Now that recycling is exercised daily, and included in the occupation one has, let's contemplate how to set a superb example. Therefore, become an ambassador for recycling to illustrate the concern and positive energy a person must create for a healthier environment. Accordingly, attending functions, town meetings, school board meetings, special events, parties, graduations, and other gatherings can open the door for a few words to encourage recycling and its significance. The approach can be laid-back in nature, with a chance to bring light on the subject. The three techniques can be done with a positive attitude and holding accountability for the actions of yourself when recycling, is the key. However, saying and giving advice is one factor, but doing the action is another component of setting a courteous example for recycling.

RECYCLING

Right now, while reading this e-book, you're probably tired of hearing about Recycle! Recycle! Recycle! However, making it to this point, one can honestly say that the task is not that difficult to carry out. Nevertheless, the main reason for the topic is not intended to command or mandate the actions of a person to recycle. Conversely, including enjoyment, a light-hearted approach, a free-spirited nature, and abundant experience into recycling is the focus. A person can do simple tasks to recycle every day. Recycling should not feel like an overwhelming duty to carry out. Simply utilizing the three procedures of reducing, reuse, and recycle can generate a transformation in the environment. Not only applying the methods of recycling but being responsible for the actions of yourself when handling trash is probably an imperative aspect to honor recycling. Some people have tendencies to be nonchalant in life about topics or subjects of importance, but not falling in that category can also exemplify an example for recycling and the like-minded approach from others that care will create a positive change in the community a person lives in when recycling is done.

OCCUPATIONAL RECYCLING

Most Americans have a typical nine to five job that they love doing I would assume. From construction, farming, teaching, doctor, a lawyer name it, people can have work-related obligations that one attends every day. People love doing their jobs and a few may not. Ultimately, bills have the last say. Paying them is a must, and the process continues every month. Contemplate about recycling at the job one works at. Also, ponder about methods that one can incorporate at the job. Whatever the field of work one is doing, seize the time to practice recycling when needed. Moreover, on lunch break or throughout the day while working, recycle the garbage or trash one has accumulated into a container made yourself that is for recycling. In addition, secure the water bottles that one has used and collect them into a trash bag. After work, drop the bag off to the nearest recycling container on the way home. Gather colleagues and coworkers together to form a recycling bin at the job, this way people know and can actively engage when recycling. Consequently, this creates a friendly atmosphere and setting examples is the focus point, overall. Nevertheless, the company or organization could be recognized for recycling initiatives which could also spread the word to other corporations to apply the same principles at their organization. However, perform those standards at your job and be that model, be that inspiration, be that person who goes the extra mile, and set an example of recycling!

BEING AN AMBASSADOR FOR RECYCLING

Yes! The sound of an ambassador can be a bit political and a large responsibility at hand. However, observe the topic from a different standpoint. Consider it as being in a leadership role or one who cares for expressing their concerns in relation to recycling. Consequently, this will diminish anxieties that may arise when trying to be a person that implores to present valuable information towards recycling. Nevertheless, there can be different avenues that a person can execute to introduce the message to the public. On the other hand, people have public speaking skills, and several lack those skills. However, practicing and figuring out what approaches can be comfortable may be the best technique. Utilize methods that may seem less different such as traveling to smaller locations such as, schools in your community, maybe the city or town hall, churches, and other whereabouts to propose information on recycling. If one can live up to the task and capable of other methods, attend meetings at state and government levels centered around ways to enhance the environment and minimize the pollution that happens every day. In addition, another method can be done to utilize the internet. Create a blog and discuss the topic or create a website and focus the page on ways for recycling. There are various other ways to portray the message, seeking that specific method can be the key to the success of how information presents itself and how being an ambassador will be successful, overall.

SETTING GOOD EXAMPLES

Overall, setting positive examples can be the right tone for just about anything when getting a job done. Moreover, as an active parent, teacher, or person who can be in a position of authority, a worthy example of being the best trickles down into the eyes of people being supervised and people in general. Therefore, adding recycling into the mixture should not be a problem at all when applying the three methods illustrated in this e-book to everyday life. Accordingly, the same initiative, determination, drive, and energy for other activities spent time on, can also be duplicated when setting an example of recycling. It is not difficult, reserve a minute to scroll through the e-book and browse a chapter or two to clear up misunderstandings towards recycling. As mentioned in this chapter, being an ambassador for recycling, applying occupational recycling, and recycling, in general, can help create a difference in the community, town, village, or city one lives in. Nevertheless, if this e-book happens to be in your hands right now, start today by protecting your community, challenging global climate change, safeguarding water resources, making recycling your friend, forming an interesting club, and lastly setting an excellent example so others can participate in creating a wonderful environment!

AUTHOR PAGE

My name is Anthony Andrew Jackson and I am pretty much laid back and reserve in nature. During my leisure time, I enjoy reading, writing, and many other activities that keep me active. Some activities include riding bikes, hiking, traveling, camping, and I can not forget about fishing! I am a father of an amazing son full of energy that also keeps me busy as well. Hopefully, this simple guide can bring you some enjoyable experiences and understanding of creating a better environment!

Contact Information

Email:
anthony.jackson454@gmail.com

www.ingramcontent.com/pod-product-compliance
Lightning Source LLC
Chambersburg PA
CBHW051422250726
48655CB00003B/1187